MW00598045

THIS BOOK BELONGS TO:

_____

_____

_____

My Bible Study Journal

© My Bible Study Journal. All rights reserved. No part of this publication may be reproduced, distributed, or transmitted, in any form or by any means, including photocopying, recording, or other electronic or mechanical methods, without prior written permission of the publisher, except in the case of brief quotations embodied in critical reviews and certain other noncommercial uses permitted by copyright law.

[Introduction]

This bible study journal is a keepsake journal to record your Bible study notes and teachings. It holds 3 months of daily journaling pages that are intentionally laid out into three sections to cultivate your relationship with God as you study the Word. Each journaling page includes a section for "Scripture", "Notes & Reflection", and then "Prayer & Praise". In the section titled "Scripture", it is recommended that you write down the Scripture passage that you are studying. By writing down the verse, it will help commit the verse to memory and establish a stronger connection and understanding. The "Notes & Reflection" section is a space where you can write down important aspects of the story that stand out to you and your own thoughts and reflection on the passage. And finally, the "Prayer & Praise" section is a space where you can pray over what the Lord has taught you and give thanks. You can also use this space to write down your daily prayer requests. We truly hope this simple and beautifully designed journal enriches your quiet time in the Word!

grace

UPON

grace

DATE:

[Scripture]

_____

_____

_____

_____

_____

[Notes & Reflection]

_____

_____

_____

_____

_____

_____

_____

_____

_____

_____

_____

_____

_____

_____

[Prayer & Praise]

_____

_____

_____

_____

DATE:

[Scripture]

_____
_____
_____
_____

[Notes & Reflection]

_____
_____
_____
_____
_____
_____
_____
_____
_____
_____
_____
_____

[Prayer & Praise]

_____
_____
_____
_____

DATE:

[Scripture]

_____
_____
_____
_____
_____

[Notes & Reflection]

_____
_____
_____
_____
_____
_____
_____
_____
_____
_____
_____
_____
_____
_____
_____
_____

[Prayer & Praise]

_____
_____
_____
_____

DATE:

[Scripture]

_____
_____
_____
_____
_____

[Notes & Reflection]

_____
_____
_____
_____
_____
_____
_____
_____
_____
_____
_____
_____
_____

[Prayer & Praise]

_____
_____
_____
_____

DATE:

[Scripture]

_____
_____
_____
_____
_____

[Notes & Reflection]

_____
_____
_____
_____
_____
_____
_____
_____
_____
_____
_____
_____
_____
_____
_____

[Prayer & Praise]

_____
_____
_____
_____

DATE:

[Scripture]

_____
_____
_____
_____
_____

[Notes & Reflection]

_____
_____
_____
_____
_____
_____
_____
_____
_____
_____
_____
_____
_____

[Prayer & Praise]

_____
_____
_____
_____

DATE:

[Scripture]

_____
_____
_____
_____
_____

[Notes & Reflection]

_____
_____
_____
_____
_____
_____
_____
_____
_____
_____
_____
_____
_____

[Prayer & Praise]

_____
_____
_____
_____

DATE:

[Scripture]

_____
_____
_____
_____
_____

[Notes & Reflection]

_____
_____
_____
_____
_____
_____
_____
_____
_____
_____
_____
_____
_____

[Prayer & Praise]

_____
_____
_____
_____

DATE:

[Scripture]

_____
_____
_____
_____
_____

[Notes & Reflection]

_____
_____
_____
_____
_____
_____
_____
_____
_____
_____
_____
_____
_____

[Prayer & Praise]

_____
_____
_____
_____

DATE:

[Scripture]

_____
_____
_____
_____
_____

[Notes & Reflection]

_____
_____
_____
_____
_____
_____
_____
_____
_____
_____
_____
_____
_____
_____

[Prayer & Praise]

_____
_____
_____
_____

DATE:

[Scripture]

_____
_____
_____
_____
_____

[Notes & Reflection]

_____
_____
_____
_____
_____
_____
_____
_____
_____
_____
_____
_____
_____
_____
_____
_____

[Prayer & Praise]

_____
_____
_____
_____

DATE:

[Scripture]

_____

_____

_____

_____

_____

[Notes & Reflection]

_____

_____

_____

_____

_____

_____

_____

_____

_____

_____

_____

_____

_____

[Prayer & Praise]

_____

_____

_____

_____

EVEN SO

IT IS WELL WITH

MY

soul

DATE:

[Scripture]

_____

_____

_____

_____

[Notes & Reflection]

_____

_____

_____

_____

_____

_____

_____

_____

_____

_____

_____

_____

_____

_____

[Prayer & Praise]

_____

_____

_____

_____

DATE:

[Scripture]

_____

_____

_____

_____

_____

[Notes & Reflection]

_____

_____

_____

_____

_____

_____

_____

_____

_____

_____

_____

_____

_____

_____

[Prayer & Praise]

_____

_____

_____

_____

DATE:

[Scripture]

_____
_____
_____
_____
_____

[Notes & Reflection]

_____
_____
_____
_____
_____
_____
_____
_____
_____
_____
_____
_____
_____
_____

[Prayer & Praise]

_____
_____
_____
_____

DATE:

[Scripture]

_____

_____

_____

_____

_____

[Notes & Reflection]

_____

_____

_____

_____

_____

_____

_____

_____

_____

_____

_____

_____

_____

[Prayer & Praise]

_____

_____

_____

_____

DATE:

[Scripture]

_____

_____

_____

_____

_____

[Notes & Reflection]

_____

_____

_____

_____

_____

_____

_____

_____

_____

_____

_____

_____

_____

_____

[Prayer & Praise]

_____

_____

_____

_____

DATE:

[Scripture]

_____
_____
_____
_____
_____

[Notes & Reflection]

_____
_____
_____
_____
_____
_____
_____
_____
_____
_____
_____
_____
_____
_____
_____

[Prayer & Praise]

_____
_____
_____
_____
_____

DATE:

[Scripture]

_____
_____
_____
_____
_____

[Notes & Reflection]

_____
_____
_____
_____
_____
_____
_____
_____
_____
_____
_____
_____
_____
_____

[Prayer & Praise]

_____
_____
_____
_____

DATE:

[Scripture]

_____

_____

_____

_____

[Notes & Reflection]

_____

_____

_____

_____

_____

_____

_____

_____

_____

_____

_____

_____

_____

_____

[Prayer & Praise]

_____

_____

_____

_____

DATE:

[Scripture]

_____
_____
_____
_____

[Notes & Reflection]

_____
_____
_____
_____
_____
_____
_____
_____
_____
_____
_____
_____
_____
_____

[Prayer & Praise]

_____
_____
_____
_____

DATE:

[Scripture]

_____
_____
_____
_____
_____

[Notes & Reflection]

_____
_____
_____
_____
_____
_____
_____
_____
_____
_____
_____
_____
_____
_____

[Prayer & Praise]

_____
_____
_____
_____

DATE:

[Scripture]

_____
_____
_____
_____
_____

[Notes & Reflection]

_____
_____
_____
_____
_____
_____
_____
_____
_____
_____
_____
_____
_____
_____
_____

[Prayer & Praise]

_____
_____
_____
_____

DATE:

[Scripture]

_____
_____
_____
_____
_____

[Notes & Reflection]

_____
_____
_____
_____
_____
_____
_____
_____
_____
_____
_____
_____
_____
_____

[Prayer & Praise]

_____
_____
_____
_____

OH, HOW HE

loves

US

DATE:

[Scripture]

_____
_____
_____
_____
_____

[Notes & Reflection]

_____
_____
_____
_____
_____
_____
_____
_____
_____
_____
_____
_____
_____
_____

[Prayer & Praise]

_____
_____
_____
_____

DATE:

[Scripture]

_____
_____
_____
_____
_____

[Notes & Reflection]

_____
_____
_____
_____
_____
_____
_____
_____
_____
_____
_____
_____
_____

[Prayer & Praise]

_____
_____
_____
_____

DATE:

[Scripture]

_____
_____
_____
_____
_____

[Notes & Reflection]

_____
_____
_____
_____
_____
_____
_____
_____
_____
_____
_____
_____
_____
_____

[Prayer & Praise]

_____
_____
_____
_____

DATE:

[Scripture]

_____
_____
_____
_____
_____

[Notes & Reflection]

_____
_____
_____
_____
_____
_____
_____
_____
_____
_____
_____
_____
_____
_____

[Prayer & Praise]

_____
_____
_____
_____

DATE:

[Scripture]

_____
_____
_____
_____
_____

[Notes & Reflection]

_____
_____
_____
_____
_____
_____
_____
_____
_____
_____
_____
_____
_____
_____
_____

[Prayer & Praise]

_____
_____
_____
_____

DATE:

[Scripture]

_____
_____
_____
_____
_____

[Notes & Reflection]

_____
_____
_____
_____
_____
_____
_____
_____
_____
_____
_____
_____
_____

[Prayer & Praise]

_____
_____
_____
_____

DATE:

[Scripture]

_____
_____
_____
_____
_____

[Notes & Reflection]

_____
_____
_____
_____
_____
_____
_____
_____
_____
_____
_____
_____
_____
_____
_____

[Prayer & Praise]

_____
_____
_____
_____

DATE:

[Scripture]

_____
_____
_____
_____
_____

[Notes & Reflection]

_____
_____
_____
_____
_____
_____
_____
_____
_____
_____
_____
_____
_____

[Prayer & Praise]

_____
_____
_____
_____

DATE:

[Scripture]

_____
_____
_____
_____
_____

[Notes & Reflection]

_____
_____
_____
_____
_____
_____
_____
_____
_____
_____
_____
_____
_____
_____
_____

[Prayer & Praise]

_____
_____
_____
_____

DATE:

[Scripture]

_____
_____
_____
_____
_____

[Notes & Reflection]

_____
_____
_____
_____
_____
_____
_____
_____
_____
_____
_____
_____
_____
_____

[Prayer & Praise]

_____
_____
_____
_____

DATE:

[Scripture]

_____
_____
_____
_____
_____

[Notes & Reflection]

_____
_____
_____
_____
_____
_____
_____
_____
_____
_____
_____
_____
_____

[Prayer & Praise]

_____
_____
_____
_____

DATE:

[Scripture]

_____
_____
_____
_____
_____

[Notes & Reflection]

_____
_____
_____
_____
_____
_____
_____
_____
_____
_____
_____
_____
_____

[Prayer & Praise]

_____
_____
_____
_____

GOD IS

good

ALL THE TIME

DATE:

[Scripture]

_____
_____
_____
_____
_____

[Notes & Reflection]

_____
_____
_____
_____
_____
_____
_____
_____
_____
_____
_____
_____
_____

[Prayer & Praise]

_____
_____
_____
_____

DATE:

[Scripture]

_____
_____
_____
_____
_____

[Notes & Reflection]

_____
_____
_____
_____
_____
_____
_____
_____
_____
_____
_____
_____
_____
_____

[Prayer & Praise]

_____
_____
_____
_____

DATE:

[Scripture]

_____

_____

_____

_____

_____

[Notes & Reflection]

_____

_____

_____

_____

_____

_____

_____

_____

_____

_____

_____

_____

_____

_____

_____

[Prayer & Praise]

_____

_____

_____

_____

DATE:

[Scripture]

_____
_____
_____
_____
_____

[Notes & Reflection]

_____
_____
_____
_____
_____
_____
_____
_____
_____
_____
_____
_____
_____
_____

[Prayer & Praise]

_____
_____
_____
_____

DATE:

[Scripture]

_____

_____

_____

_____

_____

[Notes & Reflection]

_____

_____

_____

_____

_____

_____

_____

_____

_____

_____

_____

_____

_____

_____

[Prayer & Praise]

_____

_____

_____

_____

DATE:

[Scripture]

_____
_____
_____
_____
_____

[Notes & Reflection]

_____
_____
_____
_____
_____
_____
_____
_____
_____
_____
_____
_____
_____

[Prayer & Praise]

_____
_____
_____
_____

DATE:

[Scripture]

_____
_____
_____
_____
_____

[Notes & Reflection]

_____
_____
_____
_____
_____
_____
_____
_____
_____
_____
_____
_____
_____
_____

[Prayer & Praise]

_____
_____
_____
_____

DATE:

[Scripture]

_____
_____
_____
_____
_____

[Notes & Reflection]

_____
_____
_____
_____
_____
_____
_____
_____
_____
_____
_____
_____
_____
_____

[Prayer & Praise]

_____
_____
_____
_____

DATE:

[Scripture]

_____
_____
_____
_____
_____

[Notes & Reflection]

_____
_____
_____
_____
_____
_____
_____
_____
_____
_____
_____
_____
_____

[Prayer & Praise]

_____
_____
_____
_____

DATE:

[Scripture]

_____
_____
_____
_____
_____

[Notes & Reflection]

_____
_____
_____
_____
_____
_____
_____
_____
_____
_____
_____
_____
_____

[Prayer & Praise]

_____
_____
_____
_____

DATE:

[Scripture]

_____
_____
_____
_____
_____

[Notes & Reflection]

_____
_____
_____
_____
_____
_____
_____
_____
_____
_____
_____
_____
_____

[Prayer & Praise]

_____
_____
_____
_____

DATE:

[Scripture]

_____
_____
_____
_____
_____

[Notes & Reflection]

_____
_____
_____
_____
_____
_____
_____
_____
_____
_____
_____
_____
_____

[Prayer & Praise]

_____
_____
_____
_____

GREAT IS THY

faithfulness

DATE:

[Scripture]

_____
_____
_____
_____
_____

[Notes & Reflection]

_____
_____
_____
_____
_____
_____
_____
_____
_____
_____
_____
_____
_____

[Prayer & Praise]

_____
_____
_____
_____

DATE:

[Scripture]

_____
_____
_____
_____
_____

[Notes & Reflection]

_____
_____
_____
_____
_____
_____
_____
_____
_____
_____
_____
_____
_____
_____

[Prayer & Praise]

_____
_____
_____
_____

DATE:

[Scripture]

_____
_____
_____
_____
_____

[Notes & Reflection]

_____
_____
_____
_____
_____
_____
_____
_____
_____
_____
_____
_____
_____

[Prayer & Praise]

_____
_____
_____
_____

DATE:

[Scripture]

_____
_____
_____
_____
_____

[Notes & Reflection]

_____
_____
_____
_____
_____
_____
_____
_____
_____
_____
_____
_____
_____
_____

[Prayer & Praise]

_____
_____
_____
_____

DATE:

[Scripture]

_____
_____
_____
_____
_____

[Notes & Reflection]

_____
_____
_____
_____
_____
_____
_____
_____
_____
_____
_____
_____
_____
_____

[Prayer & Praise]

_____
_____
_____
_____

DATE:

[Scripture]

_____
_____
_____
_____
_____

[Notes & Reflection]

_____
_____
_____
_____
_____
_____
_____
_____
_____
_____
_____
_____
_____
_____
_____

[Prayer & Praise]

_____
_____
_____
_____

DATE:

[Scripture]

_____
_____
_____
_____
_____

[Notes & Reflection]

_____
_____
_____
_____
_____
_____
_____
_____
_____
_____
_____
_____
_____
_____

[Prayer & Praise]

_____
_____
_____
_____

DATE:

[Scripture]

_____
_____
_____
_____
_____

[Notes & Reflection]

_____
_____
_____
_____
_____
_____
_____
_____
_____
_____
_____
_____
_____
_____

[Prayer & Praise]

_____
_____
_____

DATE:

[Scripture]

_____
_____
_____
_____
_____

[Notes & Reflection]

_____
_____
_____
_____
_____
_____
_____
_____
_____
_____
_____
_____
_____
_____
_____

[Prayer & Praise]

_____
_____
_____
_____

DATE:

[Scripture]

_____
_____
_____
_____
_____

[Notes & Reflection]

_____
_____
_____
_____
_____
_____
_____
_____
_____
_____
_____
_____
_____

[Prayer & Praise]

_____
_____
_____
_____

DATE:

[Scripture]

_____
_____
_____
_____
_____

[Notes & Reflection]

_____
_____
_____
_____
_____
_____
_____
_____
_____
_____
_____
_____
_____
_____

[Prayer & Praise]

_____
_____
_____
_____

DATE:

[Scripture]

_____
_____
_____
_____
_____

[Notes & Reflection]

_____
_____
_____
_____
_____
_____
_____
_____
_____
_____
_____
_____
_____
_____

[Prayer & Praise]

_____
_____
_____
_____

pray

WITHOUT CEASING

DATE:

[Scripture]

_____
_____
_____
_____
_____

[Notes & Reflection]

_____
_____
_____
_____
_____
_____
_____
_____
_____
_____
_____
_____
_____
_____

[Prayer & Praise]

_____
_____
_____
_____

DATE:

[Scripture]

_____
_____
_____
_____
_____

[Notes & Reflection]

_____
_____
_____
_____
_____
_____
_____
_____
_____
_____
_____
_____
_____
_____

[Prayer & Praise]

_____
_____
_____
_____

DATE:

[Scripture]

_____
_____
_____
_____
_____

[Notes & Reflection]

_____
_____
_____
_____
_____
_____
_____
_____
_____
_____
_____
_____
_____
_____

[Prayer & Praise]

_____
_____
_____
_____

DATE:

[Scripture]

_____
_____
_____
_____
_____

[Notes & Reflection]

_____
_____
_____
_____
_____
_____
_____
_____
_____
_____
_____
_____
_____
_____
_____

[Prayer & Praise]

_____
_____
_____
_____

DATE:

[Scripture]

_____
_____
_____
_____
_____

[Notes & Reflection]

_____
_____
_____
_____
_____
_____
_____
_____
_____
_____
_____
_____
_____
_____
_____
_____

[Prayer & Praise]

_____
_____
_____
_____

DATE:

[Scripture]

_____
_____
_____
_____
_____

[Notes & Reflection]

_____
_____
_____
_____
_____
_____
_____
_____
_____
_____
_____
_____

[Prayer & Praise]

_____
_____
_____
_____

DATE:

[Scripture]

_____
_____
_____
_____
_____

[Notes & Reflection]

_____
_____
_____
_____
_____
_____
_____
_____
_____
_____
_____
_____
_____
_____
_____

[Prayer & Praise]

_____
_____
_____
_____

DATE:

[Scripture]

_____
_____
_____
_____
_____

[Notes & Reflection]

_____
_____
_____
_____
_____
_____
_____
_____
_____
_____
_____
_____
_____
_____

[Prayer & Praise]

_____
_____
_____
_____

DATE:

[Scripture]

_____
_____
_____
_____
_____

[Notes & Reflection]

_____
_____
_____
_____
_____
_____
_____
_____
_____
_____
_____
_____
_____

[Prayer & Praise]

_____
_____
_____
_____

DATE:

[Scripture]

_____
_____
_____
_____
_____

[Notes & Reflection]

_____
_____
_____
_____
_____
_____
_____
_____
_____
_____
_____
_____
_____
_____
_____

[Prayer & Praise]

_____
_____
_____
_____

DATE:

[Scripture]

_____
_____
_____
_____
_____

[Notes & Reflection]

_____
_____
_____
_____
_____
_____
_____
_____
_____
_____
_____
_____
_____
_____
_____

[Prayer & Praise]

_____
_____
_____
_____

DATE:

[Scripture]

_____
_____
_____
_____
_____

[Notes & Reflection]

_____
_____
_____
_____
_____
_____
_____
_____
_____
_____
_____
_____
_____
_____

[Prayer & Praise]

_____
_____
_____
_____

PRAISE GOD
FROM WHOM ALL
blessings
FLOW

DATE:

[Scripture]

_____
_____
_____
_____
_____

[Notes & Reflection]

_____
_____
_____
_____
_____
_____
_____
_____
_____
_____
_____
_____
_____

[Prayer & Praise]

_____
_____
_____
_____

DATE:

[Scripture]

_____
_____
_____
_____
_____

[Notes & Reflection]

_____
_____
_____
_____
_____
_____
_____
_____
_____
_____
_____
_____
_____

[Prayer & Praise]

_____
_____
_____
_____

DATE:

[Scripture]

_____
_____
_____
_____
_____

[Notes & Reflection]

_____
_____
_____
_____
_____
_____
_____
_____
_____
_____
_____
_____
_____
_____

[Prayer & Praise]

_____
_____
_____
_____

DATE:

[Scripture]

_____
_____
_____
_____
_____

[Notes & Reflection]

_____
_____
_____
_____
_____
_____
_____
_____
_____
_____
_____
_____
_____
_____

[Prayer & Praise]

_____
_____
_____
_____

DATE:

[Scripture]

_____
_____
_____
_____
_____

[Notes & Reflection]

_____
_____
_____
_____
_____
_____
_____
_____
_____
_____
_____
_____
_____
_____
_____
_____

[Prayer & Praise]

_____
_____
_____
_____

DATE:

[Scripture]

_____

_____

_____

_____

_____

[Notes & Reflection]

_____

_____

_____

_____

_____

_____

_____

_____

_____

_____

_____

_____

[Prayer & Praise]

_____

_____

_____

_____

DATE:

[Scripture]

_____
_____
_____
_____
_____

[Notes & Reflection]

_____
_____
_____
_____
_____
_____
_____
_____
_____
_____
_____
_____
_____
_____
_____

[Prayer & Praise]

_____
_____
_____
_____

DATE:

[Scripture]

_____
_____
_____
_____
_____

[Notes & Reflection]

_____
_____
_____
_____
_____
_____
_____
_____
_____
_____
_____
_____
_____
_____
_____

[Prayer & Praise]

_____
_____
_____
_____

DATE:

[Scripture]

_____
_____
_____
_____
_____

[Notes & Reflection]

_____
_____
_____
_____
_____
_____
_____
_____
_____
_____
_____
_____
_____
_____
_____

[Prayer & Praise]

_____
_____
_____
_____

DATE:

[Scripture]

_____
_____
_____
_____
_____

[Notes & Reflection]

_____
_____
_____
_____
_____
_____
_____
_____
_____
_____
_____
_____
_____

[Prayer & Praise]

_____
_____
_____
_____

DATE:

[Scripture]

_____
_____
_____
_____
_____

[Notes & Reflection]

_____
_____
_____
_____
_____
_____
_____
_____
_____
_____
_____
_____
_____
_____

[Prayer & Praise]

_____
_____
_____
_____

DATE:

[Scripture]

_____
_____
_____
_____
_____

[Notes & Reflection]

_____
_____
_____
_____
_____
_____
_____
_____
_____
_____
_____
_____
_____
_____

[Prayer & Praise]

_____
_____
_____
_____

AND IF NOT

HE IS STILL

good

DATE:

[Scripture]

_____
_____
_____
_____
_____

[Notes & Reflection]

_____
_____
_____
_____
_____
_____
_____
_____
_____
_____
_____
_____
_____

[Prayer & Praise]

_____
_____
_____
_____

DATE:

[Scripture]

_____
_____
_____
_____
_____

[Notes & Reflection]

_____
_____
_____
_____
_____
_____
_____
_____
_____
_____
_____
_____
_____
_____
_____

[Prayer & Praise]

_____
_____
_____
_____

DATE:

[Scripture]

_____
_____
_____
_____
_____

[Notes & Reflection]

_____
_____
_____
_____
_____
_____
_____
_____
_____
_____
_____
_____
_____
_____

[Prayer & Praise]

_____
_____
_____
_____

DATE:

[Scripture]

_____
_____
_____
_____
_____

[Notes & Reflection]

_____
_____
_____
_____
_____
_____
_____
_____
_____
_____
_____
_____
_____
_____

[Prayer & Praise]

_____
_____
_____
_____

DATE:

[Scripture]

_____
_____
_____
_____
_____

[Notes & Reflection]

_____
_____
_____
_____
_____
_____
_____
_____
_____
_____
_____
_____
_____
_____
_____

[Prayer & Praise]

_____
_____
_____
_____

DATE:

[Scripture]

_____
_____
_____
_____
_____

[Notes & Reflection]

_____
_____
_____
_____
_____
_____
_____
_____
_____
_____
_____
_____
_____

[Prayer & Praise]

_____
_____
_____
_____

DATE:

[Scripture]

_____

_____

_____

_____

_____

[Notes & Reflection]

_____

_____

_____

_____

_____

_____

_____

_____

_____

_____

_____

_____

_____

[Prayer & Praise]

_____

_____

_____

_____

DATE:

[Scripture]

_____

_____

_____

_____

_____

[Notes & Reflection]

_____

_____

_____

_____

_____

_____

_____

_____

_____

_____

_____

_____

_____

_____

_____

[Prayer & Praise]

_____

_____

_____

_____

DATE:

[Scripture]

_____
_____
_____
_____
_____

[Notes & Reflection]

_____
_____
_____
_____
_____
_____
_____
_____
_____
_____
_____
_____
_____
_____

[Prayer & Praise]

_____
_____
_____
_____

DATE:

[Scripture]

_____
_____
_____
_____
_____

[Notes & Reflection]

_____
_____
_____
_____
_____
_____
_____
_____
_____
_____
_____
_____
_____
_____

[Prayer & Praise]

_____
_____
_____
_____

DATE:

[Scripture]

_____
_____
_____
_____
_____

[Notes & Reflection]

_____
_____
_____
_____
_____
_____
_____
_____
_____
_____
_____
_____
_____
_____
_____

[Prayer & Praise]

_____
_____
_____
_____

DATE:

[Scripture]

_____
_____
_____
_____
_____

[Notes & Reflection]

_____
_____
_____
_____
_____
_____
_____
_____
_____
_____
_____
_____
_____
_____
_____

[Prayer & Praise]

_____
_____
_____
_____

77873619R00061

Made in the USA
Columbia, SC
28 September 2017